I'M NOT CRAZY; I JUST BELIEVE GOD

Dr. Jackie Jones

ISBN: 9798987897683

DEDICATION

I first dedicate this book to the Holy Spirit, who has been my guide, inspiration, and gentle push, allowing me to find my voice and ministry and walk in my destiny.

To the countless women, men, and children I've had the pleasure of serving, inspiring, and encouraging through my many years in ministry, thank you! In turn, you have inspired and encouraged me more than words can express.

To my pastor, who gave me my first opportunity to serve the youth and women at Mount Moriah AME Church. There, I found my calling and my love for empowering women and encouraging our youth.

And I happily dedicate this book to my family—my blessings, my heartbeats, and my joy. Your love and support have made this journey possible.

TABLE OF CONTENTS

FOREWORD

I was honored when asked to write the forward for this book. I am excited about the opportunity to share my perspective on the life of this true woman of God, who leads a life that would baffle some and amaze others.

I have had the pleasure of knowing Dr. Jackie Jones since her baby girl was in the womb. At that time, it was a distant knowledge; one might label the relationship as acquaintances. To know someone requires knowledge of that person, and in acquiring knowledge, we must observe, listen, and witness an individual's life. Well, through the years, I have had the pleasure of having a front-row seat, observing a woman with a heart of gold. She puts others before herself; she encourages and edifies those who are lost and in need of direction, helping them find their way to success. She allows others to see things within themselves they never thought possible in her realm of pushing people into their gifted purpose; ah, that's it, she is a purpose pusher. She speaks truths into the lives of others, allowing their eyes to be opened to their God-given purpose. She is completely selfless as she purposes her life for betterment to ensure her abilities are endless when it comes to building prospects for others.

I envision the gift of faith over her life, which she carries well. To walk by faith, one must be bold and courageous. In Dr. Jones, I see the Prophet Elijah, wherein "The earnest prayer of a righteous person has great power and produces wonderful results." The illustration of Elijah's spoken boldness is found in 1 Kings 17:1 NLT: *"Now Elijah, who was from Tishbe in Gilead, told King Ahab, "As surely as the LORD, the God of Israel, lives-the God I serve-there will be no dew or rain during the next few years until I give the word!""*

> Elijah was as human as we are, and yet when he prayed earnestly that no rain would fall, none fell for three and a half years! Then, when he prayed again, the sky sent down rain, and the earth began to yield its crops. (James 5:17-18 NLT)

When we earnestly hear from God, believe every word that He speaks, and put those words into action, we show true faith, and this pleases God—in this, God backs every word we speak as this is His Will.

Another annotation is through the writings of

Apostle Paul in 2 Corinthians 4:13 NLT: *"But we continue to preach because we have the same kind of faith the psalmist had when he said, "I believed in God, so I spoke.""*

In Dr. Jones' delivery of the word of faith through the lives of the woman with the issue of blood, Moses raising his arms to defeat the enemy, Abraham being willing to sacrifice his son, Isaac, the many miracles of Jesus - people are convinced and convicted by those words being ministered, and they too become believers. She ministers what she wholeheartedly believes, and, therefore, she speaks. Dr. Jones being fully assured of and in the word of faith, it is illustrated through her life being just that, "faith". She does not just listen to God's Word; she does what it says by living it.

Because her walk of faith is so powerful, one might think she was crazy, not in the sense of white coat padlock crazy but more so ludicrous, ridiculous, all stemming from her gift of faith. It is written, *"If it seems we are crazy, it is to bring glory to God. And if we are in our right minds, it is for your benefit."* 2 Corinthians 5:13 NLT She continually seeks to bring glory to God in and through all things. She's not crazy, she just believes God.

I am truly proud of you, Dr. Jackie Jones; however, I'm not surprised because I know you can do all things through Christ, for He is your strength. He chose to give birth to you by giving you his true word. And you, out of all creation, became his prized possession. (James 1:18 paraphrase to personalize)

Continue living the abundant life that God has proclaimed for you (walking by faith and not by sight). You are a blessing to many, and in turn, God continues to bless you abundantly from His riches in glory. I love you.

I pray that as you read this book, you are blessed by its content and are pushed deeper into your purpose, as her push for the purpose in my life has immensely blessed me.

Marie Barrow

Marie Barrow

PREFACE

Over my many years of serving in ministry, one phrase has continually resonated with me and those I've had the privilege to serve: "I'm not crazy; I just believe God." This simple yet profound declaration has been echoed through my countless Bible studies, sermons, conferences, retreats, and various women's and church events.

"I'm not crazy; I just believe God" has become more than just words; it has become a mantra, a source of strength, and a reminder to trust God wholeheartedly, no matter how impossible the circumstances may seem. In a world that often labels faith as irrational, this phrase has inspired many to surrender fully to God and to walk in unwavering faith.

This book continues that encouragement. It reminds all who are facing challenges that seem insurmountable that with God, nothing is impossible. People may think you're crazy for stepping out in faith, but the Bible teaches us that if you have faith as small as a mustard seed, you can move mountains. So, trust in God, no matter what. You're not crazy; you're just faithful, believing in the God who can do the impossible.

INTRODUCTION

In my late teens, I was given a book that would forever change the course of my life, entitled "God's Creative Power" by Charles Capps. The pages spoke of the power of the spoken word—the incredible ability we possess to declare and decree, just as God did when He spoke the world into existence. That concept that we could speak destiny and utter words that would shape our future ignited something deep within me. It was my first introduction to what I now call crazy faith.

From that moment on, I began to live differently. I started speaking over my life with a boldness that could only come from belief in the impossible. Every declaration was a step of faith; every decree was a seed planted in the soil of destiny. God spoke, and it was. I spoke, and I believed that it would be.

This new way of living taught me that there is a power in believing beyond the natural, beyond what we can see with our eyes or understand with our minds. It taught me that crazy faith isn't about being reckless or irrational—it's about aligning our words and our hearts with God's promises, even when those promises seem impossible.

I began to see the fruit of this faith in every area of my life. Every job, every opportunity, and every encounter, I learned to walk in crazy faith, believing that what I desired, what I had declared, belonged to me. I wasn't just hoping for good things to happen; I was speaking them into existence, just as the Bible teaches us to do.

Through stories of biblical characters like the Shunammite woman, who believed in the power of a prophetic word over her life; the woman with an issue, who defied societal norms and kneeled in faith to receive her healing; and Moses, who stretched out his hand and saw the Red Sea part, I learned to walk in that same crazy faith. Their stories became my blueprint, and their victories my inspiration.

Now, every time I stand before others to minister or preach God's word, I spread the message of crazy faith. I declare it everywhere I go, teaching that we all have the power to decree and declare if we believe. If we have faith the size of a mustard seed, we can move mountains. This book, "I'm Not Crazy; I Just Believe God," is an invitation for you to join me on this journey of faith, to learn how to speak over your own life, and to discover that the impossible is within reach when you dare to believe.

CHAPTER ONE
THE TOW TRUCK MIRACLE

My car was really at the end of its lifespan. The gas gauge stopped working, and I had to estimate how much gas was in the tank and how many miles I had traveled since I last filled up at the gas station. I knew it was time for a new car, so I asked God to bless me. Nevertheless, on my way home one evening with my son and my 2-month-old daughter in the back seat, my car ran out of gas. However, running out of gas was not the dilemma. It was where I ran out of gas. I was getting onto the parkway, and as I signaled to join the oncoming cars, my car stopped. It was a really bad place to stall—a place where a collision was highly likely. Cars behind me were speeding with the expectation of merging onto the parkway and had to stop to avoid hitting me abruptly. The cars to my left were speeding along, following the traffic flow. I could feel the vibration as my car shook each time a car sped by me. I was in a bad place—a really bad place. I thought about taking the children out of the car and running to the embankment to my right, but I thought that could be dangerous. Thank God for cell phones. I called my husband and told him where I was and that I needed him to bring some gas as soon as possible. Of course, I called out to God for protection and help. And the miracle arrived, or should I say miracles.

As I was praying and awaiting my husband's arrival, a tow truck pulled up on my left side and asked if I needed help. I informed the young man in the truck that I was out of gas, and my husband was on the way. He then decided to wait next to me until my husband arrived, covering my left side from the oncoming traffic. I was genuinely appreciative and thanked God almighty. After several minutes, a second tow truck came behind me, and I saw an older tow truck driver talking to the driver waiting next to me. The second tow truck driver returned to his truck and stayed behind, covering my rear. I am totally wowed at this point as I thank God for covering and protecting myself and my family. Only God!

When a third tow truck showed up and parked in front of me to speak to the other tow truck driver, I was overcome by the unexpected and awe-inspiring nature of God's miracles surrounding me. My front, my side, and my back were all covered. It was a powerful demonstration of God's protection and His miraculous ways. That evening, God showed me that He is my protector and a miracle worker. He surrounds us with

His mercy and everlasting love. We just need to trust and believe.

My husband showed up with enough gas to get me off the next exit and to a gas station. He thanked the tow truck driver next to me, and I thanked God as I cried out loud, "I'm not crazy; I just believe God!" God showed up mighty and gave me a testimony to share with all of you. Trust him! You may find yourself in a bad place, but God is mighty and will deliver you out of any dark place. Call on him.

Jeremiah 33:3 tells us to call on the Lord, and He will answer. Don't allow fear and doubt to interfere with your miracle. Don't let the spirit of fear and doubt make you question if God heard your prayers! He did! Don't let the spirit of fear and doubt keep you in a bad place. God hears and sees all things. You have to believe in the impossible. God will provide the miracle. I'm not crazy; I just believe God.

Several women and men have also had miraculous experiences. I read about them in the Bible. Their stories have inspired me to keep believing and never give up. God loves you and will never leave you or forsake you. I am excited to share their stories with you.

CHAPTER TWO
THE WOMAN WITH AN ISSUE

Matthew 9:20-22, Mark 5:25-34, Luke 8:43-48

She is known as the woman with an issue, but she believed in God and certainly was not crazy! We learn from the scriptures that she had a blood issue. She had hemorrhaged or menstruated for 12 years. This disease rendered her unclean. As stated in the book of Leviticus 15:19–30, a woman on her menstrual cycle is considered unclean for seven days, and whoever touches her shall be unclean until that evening. Therefore, this woman must have been isolated from society. She could not be near anyone. Everything she sat on was considered unclean. Anyone who touched whatever she sat upon was expected to wash their clothes and take a bath and was considered unclean until evening. Therefore, I believe she must have lived alone and could not fully interact with her family and friends.

We learn from the scriptures that she spent all of the money she had and endured a lot of prodding and suffering from many doctors. She did not get any better but became worse. She must have felt distraught, lonely, and afraid. Knowing how unkind some people can be, she was possibly laughed at and criticized.

The woman with an issue needed a miracle, and the miracle worker was coming into her town. She heard that Jesus was passing through and decided to step out of her place of loneliness and isolation. She said, "If I could just touch the hem of his garment, I know I would be healed." My God, that is, "I'm not crazy; I just believe God," kind of faith. She stepped out of her despair, and despite the rules of uncleanliness during this time period, she made her way through the crowd. She was determined. Ignoring the stares and the sneers, she only focused on touching Jesus and her healing.

She reached up and touched the hem of his garment, and immediately, her blood disease dried up, and she felt in her body that she was healed. She refused to let the naysayers stop her. She refused to let fear stop her. She refused to let depression and despair stop her. Despite being deemed unclean and ostracized by society, she defied the norms of her time, driven by extraordinary faith that led her to believe that merely touching the hem of Jesus' garment would bring her healing. Her faith touched Jesus, and she received healing. In that amazing moment, Jesus felt her faith. He immediately turned around, asking, "Who touched me?". The woman fell on her knees and revealed herself to him. Jesus then proclaimed, "Your faith has made you whole."

This woman represents everyone with an issue. Whatever your issue may be, Jesus is the miracle worker. You just need to believe. I'm sure people thought she was crazy, but she certainly was not. She just believed God! This woman demonstrated fortitude, determination, and unwavering faith. I challenge you to give your issues to Jesus. He will heal, provide, transform, set free, and deliver. You have to believe He will, and He will! I'm Not Crazy; I Just Believe God!

CHAPTER THREE
JUST A POT OF OIL

2 Kings 4:1-7

The widow cried out to the prophet of God, Elisha. She was in great despair as her husband died and left her in significant debt. She was distraught as the creditors were on their way to take her sons into slavery as payment for the debt. After losing her husband and now about to lose her two sons to slavery, she was in utter agony. As she cried out for help, the prophet Elisha asked her a very interesting question. What do you have in your house? It is such an odd question to ask when your children are about to be taken away. She replied, "Nothing but a pot of oil." This seemingly insignificant pot of oil is a symbol of the little faith and resources we may have in times of crisis.

Amazingly, Elisha tells her to go to all her neighbors and borrow as many empty vessels and jars as she can. He tells her to go back home and, together with her sons, shut the door and pour her pot of oil into the jars she has collected. She showed faith as she followed his directives. I am sure that she could have thought to herself that this does not make any sense, but she trusted God and was obedient. She borrowed as many jars as she could gather, went home, shut the door, and started pouring.

Shutting the door is symbolic of shutting out distractions and focusing solely on God's guidance. When we put our total trust in God and operate in faith, God eliminates the distractions, creating a path of clarity to move forward in what He has assigned us to do. Distractions can interfere with your miracles. Distractions can take your focus away from God and ultimately diminish your faith. It is important to keep your focus so you can keep your faith. Shutting the door shuts out all of the naysayers and gossipers. I am sure that many of the neighbors were wondering and whispering that she must be crazy for borrowing so many empty jars. But she was not crazy. She just believed God. Her faith and obedience opened the door for her miracle.

As she began to pour the oil from her only pot into the borrowed jars, each jar started filling up with more oil. What a miracle! Her small jar of oil just kept on filling each jar she borrowed. I can imagine all of the jars and vessels filled with oil. What a sight it must have been! She believed in God's plan and kept pouring, and her faith was rewarded with a miracle. This story is a testament to the power of faith and perseverance in the face of adversity.

Once the widow had no more jars to fill, the oil stopped. She returned to Elisha, who told her to use the oil to pay off her debt and live off the rest. Not only did she pay off the debt, but she also had enough oil to sell to provide for herself and her sons. That's God's favor! When you have faith in God, you will experience God's favor! I'm not crazy; I just believe God!

CHAPTER FOUR
HE SHOWED UP IN THE FIRE

Daniel 3

There is the story of three Hebrew boys who refused to bow down and worship the image and decree of King Nebuchadnezzar. A decree was issued that when the sound of all kinds of music was heard, everyone had to bow down and worship the image of gold. Anyone who refused would be thrown into the fiery furnace. It was shared with the king that three Hebrew boys, Shadrach, Meshach, and Abednego, ignored the decree. The king was furious and called the Hebrew boys, giving them another chance to bow before him and worship. Shadrach, Meshach, and Abednego refused and declared that if they were thrown into the fire, God would deliver them, and even if He did not, they would never bow and worship false gods.

The Hebrew boys walked with incredible faith. They refused to fall into the hands of the enemy. The king was so furious that he ordered the furnace to be heated seven times hotter. Seven is the number of completion. The soldiers tied up and threw the Hebrew boys into the fire. The furnace was so hot that the flames burned the soldiers, throwing the boys into the furnace.

What fills me with awe in this story is the moment the king, peering into the furnace, sees not three but four figures walking unharmed in the fire. The king, struck by the sight, proclaims the fourth figure to be like the son of God. This part of the story makes me want to shout with joy. The king calls the boys out, and they emerge unscathed, not even smelling of smoke. The king, in awe of the God of Shadrach, Meshach, and Abednego, pays homage to Him and promotes the boys in the province of Babylon.

Hold your peace, stand, and know that God will stand with you. It takes crazy supernatural faith to stand in the midst of fire and know that God will deliver you. God will never leave you or forsake you. In the darkest hour, God will be with you! When it looks hopeless, God is with you. When you feel alone, God is with you. When you feel like you can't make it through the fire, God is with you! In your weakest moment, God is with you. You will come out unharmed, unscorched, and PROMOTED!!! I'm not crazy; I just believe God!

CHAPTER FIVE
ALL IS WELL

2 Kings 4:8-37

The prophet Elisha would often pass through the town of Shunem for ministry. A wealthy Shunamite woman urged the prophet to rest and eat at her home when he passed through town. Acknowledging that Elisha was a holy man, she asked her husband to make a room he could use when he passed through town. They made a special upper room with a bed, chair, table, and lamp. The upper room was a place of elevation, providing a place of rest and communion for God's prophet, further demonstrating that the woman made space for God's presence in her home and in her heart. Elisha wanted to show his appreciation for her kind hospitality. He asked her what she wanted. She did not have any requests, as she was content. Elisha's servant, Gehazi, shared that the Shunamite woman was without a child. The prophet declared that in one year, she would have a son.

Years later, as her son was working in the field with his father, he became sick. The boy was taken to his mother, where he died in her arms. The Shunamite woman brought her son's lifeless body into the upper room made for the prophet Elisha and laid him on the bed. Without telling her husband that their son died, she asks her husband to send a servant and a donkey so she can visit the prophet. When her husband asked, "Why would she need to visit the prophet?" Her response becomes the pinnacle of her faith: "ALL IS WELL." This phrase, 'ALL IS WELL, 'was not a denial of the situation but a declaration of her unwavering faith in God's plan. It was a powerful affirmation that she believed in God's ability to turn the situation around. She traveled approximately 20 miles to meet the prophet at Mount Carmel. After being questioned by the servant Gehazi, she again responds, "All IS WELL." She falls on her knees before the prophet Elisha and tells him about her son and that she will not leave unless he follows her back home. The woman knew her son would live when she declared, "All is well."

The prophet enters the upper room, where the body of the boy is laid upon the bed, and shuts the door. Again, "shut the door" appears in this biblical story, teaching us to shut the door on all distractions and unbelief. This act of 'shutting the door' symbolizes the need to focus on our faith and not allow doubts or distractions to interfere. It is so important that we do not allow distractions to interfere with our faith. Everyone cannot come into the room. Be mindful of those you allow in your circle. Ask the Lord to give you discernment to know who are true friends and who are fake. Your circle must have those who know how to pray with you and for you.

The prophet, Elisha, prays in the room. A man of great faith and power lies upon the boy. The man walks and continues to pray in the room, and a miracle takes place. The boy awakes!

Let's focus on the "I'm not crazy; I just believe God" faith that this Shunamite woman demonstrated. She declared in the midst of such a traumatic experience that "all is well." Although it did not look well, her faith determined it was well. Now, leaving her son, who just died in her arms, and traveling 20 miles to see the prophet takes crazy faith. This woman had faith in God that all was well and refused to accept anything else. She did not share the news with anyone. She did not need anyone to deter her faith. This woman teaches us all to stand in the midst of uncertainty and believe that the impossible is possible. Therefore, stand and declare, "All is well." It may not look well. It may not feel well. But "faith is the substance of things hoped for, the evidence of things not seen. (Hebrews 11:1). Many would have called her crazy. But I am sure her response would be, I'm not crazy; I just believe God!

CHAPTER SIX
STUCK IN THE MIDDLE

Exodus 14

Have you ever been stuck in the middle of a life-changing decision or experience? Have you ever been stuck trying to figure out your next step? Should I stay or should I go? Have you ever been in a situation where you were unable to move forward and unable to turn around and go back? Read Exodus, chapter 14; the children of Israel were stuck in the middle.

After years of living as slaves under the Egyptians, the children of Israel cried out to God for help and freedom from bondage. Their cries were answered in a way that was nothing short of miraculous. God sent Moses to lead the Israelites out of bondage. After the ten plagues God sent upon the Egyptian land, the Egyptian Pharaoh let them go. The Israelites left with everything they wanted. They plundered the Egyptians as they left Egypt. However, Pharaoh's heart was hardened. He realized no one was left to serve them. Pharaoh and his army, with chariots, pursued the Israelites to bring them back into captivity.

The children of Israel were camped at the Red Sea, and quickly approaching behind them was the Egyptian army. The children of Israel were stuck in the middle. The enemy is behind them, and an obstacle is before them. They cried out in agony. However, it is in this position that we experience the mighty miracles of God. In circumstances like these, we can cry out, "I'm Not Crazy; I Just Believe in God!"

The enemy was on horses and chariots and in pursuit. But God! God told Moses to lift up his staff. The sea divided, allowing the children of Israel to walk through the Red Sea on dry land. I loved Moses' words when he told the children of Israel, "Don't be afraid, but stand still and see the salvation of the Lord." We must remember these words when we find ourselves stuck in the middle. Standing still here doesn't mean inaction, but it's a call to trust God's plan and timing, even when uncertain and afraid. We need to remember that God loves us and will never leave us stuck in the middle. He will provide a way of escape. God will prevail if we just trust and believe in Him. We cannot allow what looks chaotic and impossible in nature to deter us from believing in a supernatural God that can make mountains move and divide seas. We cannot allow the enemy's voice to get into our minds and tell us that it is over and time to give up. With God, nothing is impossible. We just need to believe. Miracles are possible. When you don't see a way out, God is the way-maker and the miracle worker. Trust and believe in Him, and He will show you the way.

Cry out to God!! Cry out loud, watch the seas divide on your behalf, and watch the miracles open up for you! It's not a sign of weakness, but a sign of faith and reliance. This belief, this reliance, is what empowers us to face the challenges in our lives, knowing that God is with us every step of the way. I'm not crazy; I just believe God!

CHAPTER SEVEN
THE ANSWER IS KNOCKING AT THE DOOR

Acts 12:5-12

There is power in prayer, a strategy not always utilized. Prayer is our connection and communication with God! One of the followers of Christ, Peter, was in prison and scheduled to go to trial before King Herod. But the church was earnestly praying to God for Peter. Peter was bound in chains and sleeping between two soldiers. There were also soldiers in front of the prison. Suddenly, a great light appeared, and an angel appeared in the prison. The angel struck Peter on the side and raised him up. The chains fell off immediately, and the angel told Peter to get his garments and sandals and follow him. They walked past the guards and out of the prison. The angel led Peter to the city gate that opened up before them. Peter realized he was not dreaming and that an angel from God had indeed rescued him from prison. Peter then walked to Mary's house, where they were gathered in prayer, and knocked on the door. A young girl named Rhoda heard Peter's voice at the door and ran back, sharing with all those who were praying that Peter was at the door. When they opened the door and saw Peter standing before them, their astonishment turned into joy and celebration at the miraculous answer to their prayers!

The earnest prayer from the church for Peter was a powerful demonstration of faith. There is indeed power in the prayer of agreement. Miracles happen when we all come together in prayer! Everyone was praying and agreeing that Peter would be saved. An angel was sent to rescue Peter in response to the fervent prayer of the church. It is our mission to pray! It has been said over and over again that prayer changes things. When we align our faith with the word of God in agreement, there is an explosive and miraculous response. We need to trust God in our declarations of prayer. The Bible teaches us in the gospel of Matthew 18:20 that where two or three are gathered, God will be with us. Imagine the power that is illuminated when we all gather together in prayer. Our prayers become like targeted missiles directed at the subject of the request. Do not underestimate the power of your prayers, and remember the strength and unity of our faith community.

Do not lose heart if you do not see immediate results from your prayers. Remember, even faith as small as a mustard seed can move mountains. Your answer is on its way, so declare boldly, 'I'm not crazy; I just believe God!' This declaration is a testament to your unwavering faith and determination. Keep praying, keep believing, and your answer will come. The story of Peter's rescue is a powerful reminder of the importance of persistence in prayer. It is not always about the immediate results but about the unwavering faith and determination we demonstrate through our prayers. *"The prayer of a righteous person is powerful and effective"(James 5:16).* I'm not crazy; I just believe God!

CHAPTER EIGHT
FOUR FAITHFUL FRIENDS

Matthew 9:1-8, Mark 2:1-12, Luke 5:18-25

True friends stand by each other through thick and thin. They offer encouragement, companionship, enrichment, inspiration, and support. Friends celebrate life's successes and offer comfort in times of need. But when you mix all that together with faith, you have the four faithful friends who refused to deny their paralyzed friend a chance to receive a miraculous healing.

The gospels of Matthew, Mark, and Luke share this "I'm not crazy; I just believe God" story of faith. The four faithful friends heard Jesus, the miracle worker, was back in town. They immediately decided to take their paralyzed friend to Jesus, with the expectation that he would be healed. The four friends, carried their paralyzed friend on a mat to the house where Jesus was teaching. The crowd was so enormous that it was impossible to bypass and get inside the house to see Jesus. Many people would have turned around and threw in the towel. Many would have given up hope and called it a day. Some would have looked at the crowd and said, "No way." However, with their unwavering faith, the four friends refused to give up. They refused to accept the impossible. The four faithful friends climbed to the roof of the house with their paralyzed friend. They created a hole in the roof big enough and in the correct spatial position to lower the mat with their paralyzed friend right in front of Jesus! Wow, I'm not crazy; I just believe God! Jesus saw the unwavering faith of the four friends and their paralyzed friend. Jesus said to the paralyzed friend, "Your sins are forgiven. Jesus tells him to take up his mat and go home! Immediately, he stood up and went home, praising God."

We cannot allow what we see with our natural eyes to deter us from seeing the miracle. Put on your supernatural eyesight and see beyond the natural. Stop settling, because it looks impossible. So many people give up too easily and miss the miracle. I love the cliche, "Where there is a will, there is a way." Keep hoping and PUSH (Pray/Praise Until Something Happens) because it will happen if you do not give up. Remember, it's not about being crazy. It's about believing in God and the power of faith and perseverance. So, don't give up, keep pushing! The key is to keep pushing, keep believing, and never give up. I'm not crazy; I just believe God!

CHAPTER NINE
LOVE AND REDEMPTION

The Book of Ruth

During a season of drought and famine in the land of Judah, Naomi, her husband Elimelek, and their two sons traveled to Moab, where the land was fertile. Naomi's sons married Moabite women. Ruth was a young Moabite woman who married one of Naomi's sons. Within ten years of her marriage, Ruth and her mother-in-law and sister-in-law, Orpah, became widows. Naomi decided to return to Judah and encouraged her daughters-in-law to return to their mothers' homes with the hope of remarrying. Her daughter-in-law, Orpah, kissed Naomi goodbye. But Ruth replied with what becomes a very popular line repeated many times in sermons and bible stories (Ruth 1:16–17): "Don't urge me to leave you or to turn back from you." "Where you go, I will go, and where you stay, I will stay." "Your people will be my people, and your God my God." Ruth's unwavering faith, her decision to follow her mother-in-law to a place she had never known, and her belief in a purpose for her future all inspire us with the power of faith and determination.

After Ruth and Naomi returned to Judah, Ruth supported her mother-in-law and would rise early in the morning to follow behind the harvesters in the fields to gather leftover grain. Ruth did not realize that she had just happened to glean in the field belonging to Boaz, a close relative of the Elimelek family. This was not a coincidence but a part of God's plan! When you have faith, God responds, and His plan unfolds in miraculous ways!

Boaz heard of Ruth's faith and loyalty to her mother-in-law and blessed her with favor and protection. He invited Ruth to eat with him and arranged for her to gather extra grain. Ruth believed in God's provision, and God indeed opened the door for love, favor, miracles, and redemption.

Naomi knew that Boaz was a relative and, according to Jewish law, had a right to marry Ruth after the death of her husband. Ruth listened to the wisdom of her mother-in-law, who told her to put on her best clothes and go to the threshing floor, where Boaz would fall asleep protecting his harvest. Naomi instructed Ruth to uncover his feet as he slept and to lay at his feet. When Boaz awoke, he saw Ruth at his feet. She explained that he is a relative and, therefore, a guardian-redeemer. She presented herself as eligible for marriage. Boaz admired her appeal for Kinsman's redemption and assured to support her. Boaz then met with another relative who was closer in line to marry Ruth. Once that relative showed no interest, Boaz married Ruth. Boaz becomes the guardian-redeemer! He bought back Naomi's land and fathered a son to keep the family line alive. Boaz and Ruth gave birth to Obed, and Naomi became a grandmother. This is a story of love and redemption, a testament to God's great provision and control over all things. Ruth, a Moabite widow and foreigner, pledged her love and faith to God and was redeemed.

Remain faithful. God has a plan. The situation may look hopeless, but don't give up. Keep pressing. Ruth gleaned in the field every day. She was humble and determined. She did not know that Boaz was watching and admiring her tenacity. I believe Boaz fell in love with Ruth because of her faith and determination to keep moving, no matter the circumstances. I encourage you not to focus on yesterday. Keep looking up and forward. Ruth and Naomi experienced trauma, but Ruth taught us not to get stuck in the trauma. Have faith, and believe that God has a plan! God will not leave you. Keep the faith and keep moving forward. Ruth exemplifies courage. God can take a negative situation and turn it into something positive. This is a story of hope and restoration.

Ruth gave birth to a son named Obed, who is the father of Jesse, who is the father of King David! Ruth's name is mentioned in Matthew's gospel in the genealogy of Jesus Christ! Oh my! Now, this is a redemption love story that depicts that I'm not crazy; I just believe God!

CHAPTER TEN
GOD HAS A PLAN

The Book of Esther

During the reign of King Ahasuerus (also called King Xerxes), feasts and celebrations were common. During one of the banquets, King Ahasuerus requested that Queen Vashti parade before the men at the feast wearing her crown. He wanted to show off her beauty. Queen Vashti refused. To avoid her blatant refusal becoming a show of disrespect from other women throughout the kingdom, he proclaimed that Queen Vashti was no longer welcome in his presence. The search for a new queen for the king began. Hundreds of young women were taken from all of the provinces as possible candidates for the king. A young Jewish girl named Esther was among those taken. Esther was beautiful. Esther won favor with all who saw her. Esther found favor with the eunuch Hegai, who was overseeing the young women as they awaited their turn to visit with the king. The eunuch, Hegai, gave her the best room in the harem and advised her what to bring to the king during her visit.

Esther's journey to becoming the Queen of Persia was not the path she had anticipated. It was a series of unexpected events that led her to this position. Sometimes, we may find ourselves in situations and circumstances that we did not plan for. But God had a plan. God had a plan for Esther. I call it the divine setup!

Esther's father and mother died, and her cousin Mordecai raised her as his own daughter. Mordecai told Esther not to reveal her Jewish heritage because Haman, one of the kings' high advisors, hated the Jews. Haman was a descendant of Agag, who was the king of the Amalekites and an enemy of the Jewish people. Haman despised Mordecai and wanted to punish him because he refused to bow before him. Haman used his access to the king and subtly talked the king into signing a decree to destroy all of the Jews in the kingdom. There was great chaos and sorrow across the provinces. But God had a plan. There was a young Jewish girl who was now the Queen of Persia. Mordecai pleaded with Esther to do something. Esther was afraid. It was forbidden for anyone to see the king without an invitation. Anyone who approaches the king without being summoned is put to death. But Mordecai uttered what would become a popular phrase and sermon topic: "suppose you were put in this position for such a time as this" (Esther 4:14). God may place you in situations where you become a blessing to someone in need, or God may put someone in your life to bless you. I do not believe in coincidences. God is the divine orchestrator. Just like Ruth, who just happened to glean in the fields belonging to Boaz, Esther, a young Jewish girl, becomes queen and is in a position to save her people from annihilation.

It takes crazy faith to step up and go against the norm of society. Esther had to go before the king uninvited. This move could have caused her imminent death. But she believed that she was in this position for such a time as this. It takes "I'm not crazy; I just believe God" faith to walk in your purpose. It takes "I'm not crazy; I just believe God" faith to walk into unfamiliar territory. It takes "I'm not crazy; I just believe God" faith to be a risk-taker. It takes crazy faith to stand against the odds, and Esther demonstrated that faith!

Esther called the Jews to a fast and uttered, "If I perish, I perish." That's crazy faith! She approached the king, and he welcomed her in a favorable way. Esther invited both the king and Haman to a banquet. After two nights of banquets, she revealed Haman's plot to kill her people, which infuriated the king. He then had Haman killed and signed another decree that the Jews had the right to defend themselves against anyone who tried to kill them. This resulted in a victory for the Jews. Esther's faith help save her people. Mordecai was also promoted to second in command to the king and held in high esteem.

Step out in faith, no matter what it looks like. Don't allow fear to hold you back from your destiny. Don't allow the negativity of others to prevent you from reaching your goals and fulfilling your dreams. You were born for a purpose. You are where you are now because you have a purpose to fulfill. It may not look like what you expected, but hold on. Your reward is coming! Your victory is in your faith. You have to believe it will work in your favor. God has the final say. It is all in the plan. It may not make sense, but God has a plan. I'm not crazy; I just believe God!

CHAPTER ELEVEN
FROM FEAR TO FAITH

Judges 6-8

Gideon, a man who saw himself as the least in his family, from the weakest clan in Manasseh, was chosen by God to deliver Israel from the oppressive hold of the Midianites. The Midianites and other eastern people would steal and destroy Israel's crops and livestock. The Israelites succumbed to living in caves and mountain clefts. Gideon seemed the least likely candidate for such a mighty task, and his response was rooted in fear and inadequacy. Gideon's story demonstrates how God calls the unlikely and equips them for greatness.

The angel of the Lord appeared to Gideon and called him a "mighty warrior." If I could read Gideon's mind, I'm sure Gideon thought that the angel must have been crazy. He questioned the very call, asking, "*How can I save Israel? My clan is the weakest in Manasseh, and I am the least in my family*" (see Judges 6:15-16). Gideon is wrestling with the thoughts that so many people face: feelings of unworthiness and insignificance. These thoughts of negativity can be paralyzing. They keep us bound, unable to step into the fullness of what God has prepared for us. Like Gideon, many people believe that their prayers are insignificant, that they are not ready or worthy to be all God has called them to be. Well, that is a lie! God, in His infinite wisdom, sees you differently. He sees beyond your limitations and fears. Just like the story of the crippled woman in the Gospel of Luke 13:10–17; the woman was bent over for 18 years. On the day when Jesus was teaching, he saw her in the back of the synagogue and called her to him, and in the end, he healed her, and everything that weighed her down no longer was a hindrance. God sees you! Just like the young shepherd boy David, who was in the field tending to the sheep, the youngest brother, the least expected, was the one anointed and appointed to be the king of Israel. He sees the mighty warrior within each of us, ready to rise above every challenge. He specializes in using the weak and the fearful to accomplish His purposes. In God's hands, our inadequacies become opportunities for His strength to be displayed. The truth is, with God on our side, anything is possible.

The angel of the Lord assured Gideon that he would be with him and that he would destroy all of the Midianites. Interestingly, Gideon asked for a sign to be sure that it was truly the Lord, and when he recognized that, indeed, he was face-to-face with an angel, he knew he was not crazy; he believed God! The Bible tells us that the Spirit of the Lord came upon Gideon. Gideon defeats the Midianites. But the strategy God used is what I call "I'm not crazy; I just believe God" faith. Gideon gathered an army of troops to strike the Midianites, but God told him that his army of 32,000 troops was too large. God told Gideon with that large number, Israel's army would take the credit; God wanted to demonstrate His mighty and miraculous power! God instructed Gideon to send home men who were afraid. This reduced the number to 10,000. God again indicated that the army was too large. Then God further reduced the troops by selecting those who drank water at the river in a certain manner, which left Gideon with just 300 men. God then allowed Gideon to overhear a Midianite soldier sharing a dream that, when interpreted, declared Gideon's victory over the Midianites. Gideon was encouraged and confident to go into battle! The amazing "I'm not crazy; I just believe God" strategy used to fight this battle was a miracle in itself. Gideon and his army of 300 men surrounded the Midianite camp, each holding a trumpet and a torch inside a jar! God often uses strategies that defy human logic; I call these strategies miracles! When Gideon gave the signal, the men all blew their trumpets, broke the jars, and held the torches with their left hand. God fought the battle. God had the Midianites turn their swords against each other. It was utter chaos. The Midianites slew the Midianites. God will fight your battles! No matter what you are facing, turn it over to God and trust God with all your heart. It takes crazy faith, and crazy faith is victorious.

Gideon stepped out of his place of inadequacy and gave God a yes. Give God a yes and let it go. Faith will fight your battles; crazy faith will win the war! This little boy saw himself as insignificant and unworthy, yet God called him to save a nation! I'm not crazy; I just believe God! The same God who empowered Gideon to lead a small band of 300 men to victory over a large Midianite army is the same God who walks with us today. One of the greatest challenges we face as believers is knowing who we are in Christ and truly understanding who God is. When we don't fully accept our identity in Christ, we struggle to fulfill our purpose and calling in life. We see ourselves through the lens of our insecurities rather than through the truth of God's Word. Gideon's journey from fear to faith teaches us that it's not just about who we are but about who God is. It's about trusting in His power and His plan to work through us despite our weaknesses. The pressures of life can often make us lose sight of who we are. They can warp our vision and lead us to believe that we are less than what God has made us to be.

The story of Gideon reminds us that in our weakest moments, God is powerful. He calls us not because of our qualifications but because of His purpose and plan. In each of us, there is a special plan and destiny. In each of us, there is a mighty warrior waiting to be fulfilled. Don't sit on your gift! Don't let anyone define you. Sometimes, we can get in our own way! Recognize the power that is within you! As believers, it's crucial that we reject the lies of inadequacy and insignificance. We must stand above the thoughts of negativity that seek to pull us down and instead embrace the truth of who we are in Christ. We are chosen and equipped by God to do great things. The gifts He has given us are not to be hidden but to be used to build His kingdom and to live lives of joy and abundance. The Apostle Matthew said it this way, "You're here to be light, bringing out the God-colors in the world. God is not a secret to be kept. We're going public with this, as public as a city on a hill" (see Matthew 5:14-16 MSG).

Gideon's story is a call to rise above our inadequacy and societal negativity, to see ourselves as God sees us, and to step boldly into the purpose He has for us. Just as Gideon went from hiding in fear to leading a nation to victory, so can we move from doubt to destiny. With God, we are more than conquerors, and there is no challenge too great, no obstacle too insurmountable, and no dream too impossible when we stand firm in our identity in Him. I'm not crazy; I just believe God!

CHAPTER TWELVE
WHAT DO YOU SEE

2 Kings 6

The Israelites were at war with the king of Aram. However, every time the king of Aram declared a plan to attack Israel, the prophet Elisha would send a warning. The king's plan was always foiled. The king of Aram heard that the prophet Elisha was responsible for warning Israel. Upon finding out the whereabouts of Elisha, the king sent horses and chariots and surrounded the city with the intent to capture Elisha.

Elisha's servant, Gehazi, arose in the morning and immediately saw that the city was surrounded. He cries out to Elisha in fear! I love Elisha's response. He declared, "Don't be afraid: "Those who are with us are more than those who are with them." I am sure Gehazi looked at Elisha like he was crazy, but Elisha was not crazy at all. He just believed in God! Elisha prayed to the Lord to open Gehazi's eyes so that he could see! I so love this miracle. The Lord answered and opened Gehazi's eyes, and in the hills, he saw an army of angels and horses and chariots of fire surrounding the enemy. WOW! What a miracle! God allowed Gehazi to see into the spirit realm. We live in the natural world. But there is a spirit realm with angels assigned to protect and answer our prayers. The enemy was outnumbered. There are situations that you may find yourself in that may look grim. But there is a God that is telling you, "Don't be afraid." God will send angels to your rescue.

Imagine waking up in the morning and seeing an army surrounding you, ready to capture you. The prophet, Elisha, was so calm. He knew an army of protection surrounded the enemy and was ready to hold them captive. We need to recognize that we are never alone. God is always with us. Elisha prayed to the Lord to strike the army with blindness and led the army to the Israel camp in Samaria. When they reached Samaria, he prayed that their eyes would be opened. When they opened their eyes, they were now in the camp of Israel. Elisha advised the king of Israel not to kill them but to feed them and send them back home. The king of Aram stopped raiding Israel and, I am sure, recognized the power of the one and true God!

I'm not crazy; I just believe God will take care of you. God will protect, cover, guide, and keep you in peace. God will put enemies under your feet. Again, stop looking at everything with a natural lens. Put on those spiritual glasses of faith and recognize who you are in the kingdom. Walk by faith and not by sight! It's this unwavering faith that inspires us and gives us hope in the face of challenges.

Ask the Lord to open your spiritual eyes! Expect to see miracles, signs, and wonders! This call to seek spiritual insight is not a sign of craziness but a source of encouragement and motivation in our faith journey. I'm not crazy; I just believe in God!

CHAPTER THIRTEEN
EVEN NOW

John 11:1-44

Sisters Mary and Martha sent word to Jesus that their brother Lazarus was sick. Jesus stayed where he was for an additional two days, then made the two-day journey to Judea. He announced that Lazarus was dead, but he would raise him up for all to see the glory of God, demonstrating the power of faith in God's ability to overcome seemingly impossible situations.

When Jesus arrived in Judea, he was told that Lazarus had been dead in the tomb for four days. Martha ran out to meet him, crying, "If you were here, my brother would not have died." Martha demonstrated a profound faith in God's power when she proclaimed, "EVEN NOW," God would do whatever you ask. This is not a blind faith, but a faith that is rooted in the belief that God's power is not limited by time or circumstances. Lazarus has been in the tomb for four days, dead, and his sister not only believes but also recognizes that Jesus is the Messiah and has the power and authority to raise her brother from the dead. Even now, Martha believes that a miracle can take place.

In our journey called life, there may be circumstances that look dead. There may be situations that are buried and assumed to be hopeless. But with "I'm not crazy; I just believe God" faith, what you thought was dead can be resurrected! God has the final say. Just because something looks dead does not mean it is dead. All things are possible.

Jesus goes to the tomb and asks to have the stone removed from the entrance. Martha is concerned with the odor, but Jesus again talks about the glory of God! Jesus declares, "Lazarus, come forth." Lazarus comes out of the tomb wrapped in cloth, and Jesus tells them to take off the grave clothes. This miraculous event is a testament to the power of faith. Martha's unwavering belief in Jesus and his ability to perform miracles led to the resurrection of her brother. WOW, I'm not crazy; I just believe God!

It is time to resurrect that idea. It's time to resurrect that relationship. Don't be so quick to bury something that seems dead! Don't you know that you serve an even now God?

Even now, you can still pass the class. Even now, you can still get the job. Even now, you can find love. Even now, you can start over. Even now, you can still write the book. Even now, you can go back to school.

Even now, you can start the business. Even now, you can begin to travel. Even now, you can begin a new ministry. Even now, you can buy a new home. Even now, you can begin fresh, eat better, and take care of yourself. Even now, you can declare, "I'm not crazy, I just believe in an 'even now' God!"

CHAPTER FOURTEEN
IT FELL FROM THE SKY

As soon as I walked through the door and into the living room, I knew this was my home. The wood cabinets in the kitchen and the high wood ceiling called my name. I immediately spoke to God and said, This is it! As I walked off the property, I looked back and began to praise God! I started to dance victoriously in front of the house. I believe in praising God in advance. I knew this was it!

I drove back to my apartment to share the news with my husband. I was so excited! Together with the children, we visited again within the week. Everyone loved the house. We made an offer to purchase the house. However, after discussing the financial details, we realized that the house was $50,000 more than we were able to afford. My husband decided to keep looking for a home that was more affordable. Reluctantly, I continued the search. We visited several properties within the same area, but I knew that the house I visited was our new home. I suggested we visit again. After further discussion, the owners refused to decrease the price. The owner would not take a penny less than the asking price. My husband and I sat in the car and discussed taking money from our tax-deferred accounts. I knew that this was our home. The feeling I had when I first visited gave me a sense of peace and reassurance. Somehow, it had to work out in our favor. The emotional rollercoaster of hope, disappointment, and determination was exhausting, but I held onto my faith and the belief that this was the home God had chosen for us.

It was the month of February, and the money from our tax-deferred accounts would not be available until June. We decided to call the owners and ask if they were willing to wait until June to close on the property. My husband agreed that we would look no further if they said yes. Of course, the owner said yes! I recall looking up and thanking God for his favor. However, the miracle showed up after we closed and moved into our new home.

Moving into our house was exciting, but the house needed a full makeover. We needed new carpets, blinds, and a complete paint job. We put all of our savings plus more into purchasing the house and therefore had no additional money to make our house into a home. We began cleaning and clearing out non-essential items. We cleaned all of the rooms and then began to disinfect the basement. As my husband was moving one of the shelves in the basement, an envelope flew from the top of the shelf. Out of the "sky," we were looking at $5,000 in cash. Only God can do this! Only God can make money fall from the sky, in this case, the basement ceiling. But it was a true miracle. This unexpected blessing reaffirmed my faith and belief in God's providence, leading me to exclaim, "I'm not crazy; I just believe God." Immediately, we were able to purchase paint for each room and put a down payment on carpets for all of the rooms in the house. God is so amazing. What is for you is for you! We must put our trust in God. No matter the circumstances, we have to put our trust in God. The average person may not believe this story, but when you are a believer in God and walk by faith, you are certainly not average. You are blessed and highly favored. Therefore, I shout out everywhere I go, "I'm not crazy; I just believe God!

CHAPTER FIFTEEN
WALKING IN CRAZY FAITH

As we come to the end of this book but not the end of your journey, I want to leave you with a truth that has never been more urgent and more necessary. We are living in times that demand we walk in crazy faith. The world around us is marked by uncertainty, instability, and challenges that seem to grow more complex each day. The famous Apostle Paul tells us that it is not our job to conform to this world but to be transformed by renewing our minds (see Romans 12:2). We don't know what tomorrow holds, and that reality can be overwhelming. But in the midst of all this, there is one unshakable truth: If we believe in Christ and walk in crazy faith, all will be well.

We are called to walk by faith and not by sight, to trust in what we cannot see, and to believe in what seems impossible. This is not an easy path, but it is the only path that leads to peace, purpose, and the fulfillment of God's promises in our lives. No matter what it looks like around us, no matter how chaotic or uncertain the world may be, we must walk in crazy faith, knowing that God is in control and that His plans for us are good.

Now, more than ever, I urge you to deepen your relationship with the Holy Spirit, who is our comforter and teacher. Let the Holy Spirit lead you every day of your life. It takes crazy faith to listen to that still, small voice when everything around you is screaming the opposite. It takes crazy faith to surrender your plans, your fears, and your life to God. But it is this very surrender that will protect your future. We cannot navigate this world without the Holy Spirit ordering our steps, speaking to us, guiding us, and teaching us what to do. The world offers us many voices, but it is the voice of the Holy Spirit that we must follow if we are to live in victory. The Apostle John wrote a message from God that said, "*My sheep hear my voice, and I know them, and they follow me: And I give them eternal life, and they shall never perish, nor shall any man pluck them out of my hand*" (John 10:27–28). This requires a heart that is fully surrendered to God, a heart that trusts Him completely even when it doesn't make sense. It is at these moments that miracles take place. It is at these moments that we say, "I'm not crazy; I just believe God!"

As you move forward from this book, I encourage you to walk in crazy faith every day of your life. Embrace the unknown with the assurance that God is with you and that His plans for you are greater than anything you could imagine. Remember, you don't need to have all the answers; you only need faith the size of a mustard seed. That tiny seed of faith has the power to move mountains, to change the course of your life, and to bring the impossible into reality.

We don't know what tomorrow brings, but we do know the One who holds tomorrow. And if you trust in Him, if you walk in crazy faith, you will be okay. This is not just a hopeful sentiment; it is a divine promise. So, as you close this book, open your heart to God, surrender to His will, and step into the future with the confidence that comes from knowing that you are guided by the Holy Spirit and held by a God who loves you beyond measure.

You're not crazy; just walk in crazy faith, believe in the impossible, and watch as God works miracles in your life every single day. Therefore, declare it loud and proud: I'm not crazy; I just believe God!

CHAPTER SIXTEEN
TELL YOUR STORY

I'm not crazy; I just believe God Story

Write your "I'm not crazy; I just believe God" faith story.

I'm not crazy; I just believe God…

_____

_____

_____

_____

_____

_____

_____

_____

_____

I'M NOT CRAZY; I JUST BELIEVE GOD

_____

_____

_____

_____

_____

_____

_____

_____

_____

_____

_____

_____

_____

_____

_____

_____

_____

I'M NOT CRAZY; I JUST BELIEVE GOD

_____

_____

_____

_____

_____

_____

_____

_____

_____

_____

_____

_____

_____

_____

_____

_____

I'M NOT CRAZY; I JUST BELIEVE GOD

_____

_____

_____

_____

_____

_____

_____

_____

_____

_____

_____

_____

_____

_____

_____

_____

_____

_____

_____

_____

_____

_____

_____

_____

_____

_____

_____

_____

_____

_____

_____

_____

_____

_____

I'M NOT CRAZY; I JUST BELIEVE GOD

_____

_____

_____

_____

_____

_____

_____

_____

_____

_____

_____

_____

_____

_____

_____

_____

_____

_____

_____

_____

_____

_____

_____

_____

_____

_____

_____

_____

_____

_____

_____

_____

ABOUT THE AUTHOR

Dr. Jackie Jones is an inspirational speaker and minister who is passionate about encouraging men and women to live spiritual life of faith leads to strengthens me," is a retired deputy currently serving as an educational and an ordained minister. Dr. Jones also the "Faith and Favor Ministries," where she inspires audiences to discover their purpose and pursue their destiny.

s an eloquent and inspirational speaker on living faith and trusting in God, Dr. Jones travels to spread the good news to uplift and encourage her audiences to live life to the fullest, following biblical principles and promises. She desires to motivate young people and adults to fulfill their highest potential in life. Her educational background includes a Bachelor of Arts in Psychology, a Master of Arts in Special Education, a Master of Science in School Leadership, and a Doctorate in Educational Leadership. Her work often emphasizes the importance of Dialectical Behavior Therapy (DBT) in achieving balanced and fulfilled lives. She is a strong advocate in the education field with a passion for empowering vulnerable students and people of all ages.

Although Dr. Jackie Jones is called to work in wh   she thanks God daily for her first ministry,

Made
Colum
20 September

42716899R00048